CORN SNAI
ESSENTIAL (
HANDBOOK

Complete Guide to Housing, Nutrition,
Breeding, Health, Problem solving,
Bonding, Diverse Patterns and More

NORMAN T. SMITH

COPYRIGHT © 2023 BY NORMAN T. SMITH

CHAPTER ONE

INTRODUCTION

Corn snakes (Pantherophis guttatus), which are endemic to the southeastern United States, have become extremely popular as pet snakes in recent years. Their brilliant colors, placid temperament, and manageable size make them an excellent choice for both novice and seasoned reptile keepers. In this extensive examination, we will look into the history of corn snakes in the pet trade, discover why they are popular as pets, and examine their fundamental traits and behavior.

Corn snakes are members of the colubrid family, which is distinguished by their thin body and lack of venom. They are known for their striking coloration, which includes a pattern of vibrant reds, oranges, and browns that resembles maize kernels, hence the name "corn snake." Their average size ranges from 3 to 5 feet, with some individuals growing larger, making them a manageable size for most reptile enthusiasts.

Corn snakes live in a wide range of settings, from forests and grasslands to abandoned buildings. They are skilled climbers who use their abilities to look for prey and find refuge. They are mainly active throughout the evening and night as nocturnal creatures, exhibiting a habit known as crepuscular, which is common in many snake species.

Corn Snakes in the Pet Trade: A Brief History

Corn snakes first appeared in the pet sector in the late twentieth century. They were not initially as famous as they are today, but their relaxed personality and attractive beauty eventually drew notice. Captive breeding operations helped to make them more available to pet owners, lowering the demand for wild-caught individuals.

Selective breeding has also led to the wide range of color variants now available in the pet trade. Morphs are color and pattern variants that have been purposefully cultivated to improve particular features. This has led in a diverse range of corn snake morphs, from the conventional "normal" look to more exotic varieties like as albino, anerythristic, and hypo.

Why You Should Get a Corn Snake as a Pet:

Several reasons contribute to corn snakes' popularity as pets. First and foremost, they are manageable in size. Corn snakes, unlike bigger snake species, are ideal for people with little room, making them a good alternative for apartment residents or those with smaller living spaces.

Another important issue is the docility of corn snakes. Corn snakes develop acclimated to human interaction with regular handling, making them an excellent choice for inexperienced reptile keepers. Their placid demeanor and absence of venom make them a safe and entertaining family pet.

Corn snakes are also quite low-maintenance. They have simple food demands, often eating on mice or rats, and their enclosure requirements are low in comparison to certain other reptile species. These characteristics make them an appealing alternative for individuals wishing to get into reptile keeping without taking on too many obligations.

Fundamental Characteristics and Behavior:

Understanding the fundamental traits and behavior of corn snakes is critical for giving the best possible care. As previously said, their usual size ranges from 3 to 5 feet, with a slim body and a striking pattern of brilliant colors.

Corn snakes are noted for their curiosity. They often inspect their environment, using their climbing ability to investigate items and conceal in high places. To accommodate their natural behavior, a cage with branches and hides is required.

Corn snakes are carnivorous, mostly devouring rodents. The frequency of feeding is determined by the snake's age, with younger snakes requiring more frequent feedings. Nutrition is critical to their health and well-being.

It is critical that they maintain an adequate temperature gradient within their container. Corn snakes, like many other reptiles, need a thermal gradient to keep their body temperature stable. This entails providing a warm and a cold side of the enclosure, with the snake free to wander between the two as needed.

Finally, corn snakes have earned their spot as one of the most popular pet reptiles. They are a fantastic choice for both novice and seasoned reptile enthusiasts because to their manageable size, spectacular look, and placid nature. Responsible pet ownership entails knowing their natural tendencies, giving adequate care, and providing a proper living environment. Corn snakes may flourish in captivity with adequate attention and care, giving delight and curiosity to their owners for many years.

CHAPTER TWO

CREATING THE IDEAL CORN SNAKE HABITAT

Providing an ideal environment for your corn snake is critical to its health, well-being, and general enjoyment. A well-designed cage should closely resemble the snake's natural environment, including components for thermoregulation, security, and cerebral stimulation. In this comprehensive tutorial, we will look at the important components of creating the ideal corn snake environment, including enclosure selection, substrate, temperature, humidity, lighting, and enrichment.

Selecting the Best Enclosure:

When creating a corn snake habitat, the first and most important issue is choosing a suitable cage. Corn snakes are frequently housed in terrariums or glass aquariums with a lockable lid. The enclosure should be appropriate to the size of the snake to allow for comfortable mobility and thermoregulation. A 20-gallon tank is usually adequate for little snakes, but bigger snakes may need a 40-gallon or larger cage.

Ventilation is critical for preventing humidity accumulation and maintaining air circulation within the enclosure. A tight-fitting lid is critical for preventing escapes and protecting your snake from any risks. Additionally, giving a hiding place for your corn snake is essential for stress reduction. On both the warm and cool sides of the enclosure, half logs, commercial hides, or DIY shelters can be installed.

Substrate Selection and Upkeep:

Choosing a good substrate is critical for keeping your corn snake clean and comfortable. Aspen bedding is a popular choice since it allows for burrowing and helps keep humidity levels stable. Newspaper or paper towels are also useful for simple cleanup and waste monitoring.

Regular maintenance is essential for maintaining a sanitary environment. To eliminate wastes and uneaten food, spot cleaning should be done on a regular basis. To minimize bacteria and odor development, a thorough substrate replacement should be performed on a regular basis, often every 4-6 weeks. Maintaining cleanliness is critical for minimizing respiratory disorders and maintaining your corn snake's general health.

Requirements for Temperature and Humidity

Corn snakes are ectothermic, which means they rely on external heat sources to control their body temperature. It is critical for their physiological well-being to maintain a healthy temperature gradient within the cage. A heat source, such as an under-tank heating pad or heat tape, should be inserted on one side of the enclosure to provide a warm basking zone while leaving the other side chilly.

The basking area should be heated to 85-90°F (29-32°C), while the colder side should be kept at 75-80°F (24-27°C). This temperature differential enables the snake to manage its body temperature by moving between warm and cool locations.

Maintaining proper humidity levels is also critical. Corn snakes thrive at humidity levels ranging from 40-60%. This may be accomplished by providing a drinking bowl and boosting humidity through substrate selection or periodic spraying.

However, excessive humidity should be avoided because it might cause respiratory troubles and other health concerns.

Considerations for Lighting and Photoperiod

Corn snakes are not as reliant on UVB illumination as some other reptile species, but a consistent day-night cycle is still necessary for their survival. The use of a light source on a 12-hour cycle helps regulate their circadian rhythm and supports natural activities.

While natural light from a nearby window might help with their photoperiod, a steady light source in the cage is necessary. This is possible with a low-wattage incandescent bulb or an LED light. The light should be placed in such a way that it creates a day-night cycle without producing undue stress or disrupting their sleep cycles.

Options for Enrichment and Hide:

Enrichment is a key component of providing your corn snake with a stimulating habitat. While these reptiles are not as interactive as mammals, they do benefit from mental stimulation and a diversity of environments. Allowing them to display natural behaviors and relieve stress by providing hiding spaces, branches, and climbing chances.

To provide a sense of security, commercial skins, half logs, and other shelters can be strategically placed. Corn snakes are ambush predators who like to hide in order to examine their environment. Providing branches or other climbing structures also helps children to explore vertical environments, which benefits their general well-being.

Rotating and rearranging hides and enrichment items on a regular basis prevents boredom and stimulates natural behaviors. Providing a variety of textures and surfaces in the enclosure can also help to improve the snake's sensory experience.

Finally, designing the ideal corn snake habitat needs careful consideration of cage type, substrate, temperature, humidity, lighting, and enrichment. You may construct a habitat that supports your corn snake's health, comfort, and natural habits by recreating their natural environment and meeting their individual needs. A flourishing and satisfied pet will benefit from regular observation and modifications to their surroundings depending on their behavior and preferences.

CHAPTER THREE

CORN SNAKE NUTRITION AND FEEDING

Proper food and nutrition are critical for the well-being and lifespan of captive corn snakes. A well-balanced diet that mimics their normal eating patterns is critical to their overall health. Understanding the natural diet of corn snakes, selecting appropriate prey items, developing a feeding plan with adequate portion sizes, resolving frequent feeding concerns, and monitoring and maintaining a good body condition for your corn snake will all be covered in this complete book.

Understanding Corn Snakes' Natural Diet:

Corn snakes are carnivorous reptiles that eat rodents, small animals, birds, and even amphibians in their native habitat. Their diet is most efficiently duplicated in captivity by providing adequately sized and nutritionally balanced prey items. Corn snakes are constrictors, which means they squeeze their prey by wrapping their body around it. This feeding approach should be considered while picking prey items to ensure they are the right size for the snake.

Corn snakes' eating pattern may vary seasonally in their natural environments. They are more active hunters during the warmer months and may lessen their feeding frequency during the winter months. When creating a feeding regimen in captivity, keep this natural volatility in mind.

Choosing Appropriate Prey Item:

Choosing the correct prey items is critical for your corn snake's health and well-being. In captivity, the most usual prey items supplied are properly sized mice or rats. The prey should be appropriate to the snake's girth, ensuring that it is neither too little to supply enough nourishment nor too huge to cause regurgitation.

Prey items can be bought frozen and thawed before being offered, or live prey can be utilized if preferred. However, live prey poses a greater danger of damage to the snake and should be properly observed while feeding. To minimize inadvertent bites when feeding, it is usual practice to offer the prey to the snake with tongs.

To promote nutritional variety, it is critical to provide a diversified diet. Feeding your corn snake a range of prey items, including different sizes and types of rodents, adds to a more balanced nutritional profile.

Portion sizes and feeding schedule:

Establishing a regular feeding regimen is critical for your corn snake's health and well-being. Younger snakes require more regular feedings, usually every 5-7 days, however adult snakes can be fed every 10-14 days. It's critical to pay attention to your snake's particular demands, changing the feeding plan based on its size, age, and overall health.

The size of the prey item should correspond to the snake's size. As a general guideline, give prey items that are around the same width as the snake's widest section. Overeating can result in obesity and other health problems, whereas undereating can result in malnutrition and stunted growth.

It is important to carefully observe your snake's behavior and bodily condition in order to determine the sufficiency of the feeding plan. A healthy snake will have a balanced body shape with a moderate taper from head to tail. Weighing your snake on a regular basis and changing meal proportions accordingly aids in maintaining a healthy weight.

Feeding Problems and Solutions:

Feeding difficulties may develop despite good preparation. Common issues that snake owners may face include refusal to feed, vomiting, and trouble shedding. These problems can be due to a variety of circumstances, such as stress, improper temperatures, disease, or feeding prey that is too large.

Consider environmental changes, recent handling, or the mating season if your snake refuses to eat. Providing a peaceful and safe eating space, as well as lowering stresses, can help to stimulate appetite. If the problem persists, see a reptile veterinarian to rule out any underlying health issues.

Regurgitation is a more significant condition that might be caused by overfeeding, incorrect temperatures, or an underlying health concern. Allowing the snake time to recuperate after regurgitation is critical before attempting to feed again. Address any environmental or husbandry difficulties, and seek veterinary treatment if problems continue.

Inadequate humidity might cause difficulty shedding or retained shed. Maintaining a good shedding environment through the use of a humidity box or regular misting aids in the shedding process. If your snake is frequently shedding, humidity conditions in the enclosure may need to be adjusted.

Monitoring and Maintaining Physical Fitness:

Regular body condition monitoring of your corn snake is critical for avoiding and resolving possible health concerns. A healthy snake should have a distinct body form that is neither too skinny nor overly round. Weighing your snake on a regular basis and maintaining a food diary allows you to watch its growth and change feeding regimens accordingly.

Maintaining a suitable body condition is critical for your corn snake's general health and lifespan. Obesity can cause a number of health problems, including fatty liver disease and a shorter lifespan. Underfeeding, on the other hand, can lead to stunted development, reproductive problems, and reduced immunological function.

Regular health check-ups with a reptile veterinarian are suggested in addition to checking bodily condition. A veterinarian may advise on diet, diagnose possible health concerns, and provide preventative care suggestions.

Finally, feeding and nourishment are critical components of responsible corn snake ownership. Understanding their natural diet, selecting appropriate prey items, arranging a feeding plan, resolving frequent feeding concerns, and checking body condition are all important factors in preserving your corn snake's health and well-being. You may contribute to a happy and successful pet snake for years to come by giving a balanced and varied diet as well as careful care.

CHAPTER FOUR

HEALTH CARE AND COMMON ISSUES IN CORN SNAKES

Caring for a corn snake entails not only providing a suitable home and sustenance, but also monitoring their health. Regular health checks, being aware of the symptoms of a healthy snake, identifying common health concerns, implementing preventative care measures, locating a reliable reptile veterinarian, and knowing emergency protocols are all important components of responsible corn snake ownership.

Regular Health Examinations and Symptoms of a Healthy Corn Snake:

Regular health checks are an important part of keeping your corn snake healthy. These tests include observing their behavior, appearance, and monitoring their environment. The following are signs of a healthy corn snake:

A healthy corn snake is typically active, exploring its environment and engaging in regular habits like basking, hunting, and shedding.

Clear Eyes: The eyes of the snake should be clear, with no cloudiness, discharge, or swelling.

Healthy skin should be smooth and devoid of wounds, bumps, and discolouration. Shedding should happen in one piece without trouble.

Clear Nose and Mouth: There should be no discharge or symptoms of respiratory difficulties in the nose or mouth.

Body form: The snake's body form should be well-defined, neither too thin nor overly round. Weighing the snake on a regular basis allows you to keep track of its development and overall condition.

Regular Eating Habits: A healthy snake should have a steady hunger and feed normally.

Any changes from these signals may suggest a possible health risk, and fast attention is critical for resolving problems as they arise.

Common Corn Snake Health Problems:

While corn snakes are typically tough, they are vulnerable to some health problems. Understanding these difficulties is critical for early identification and action. Corn snakes commonly suffer from the following health problems:

Wheezing, open-mouth breathing, and nasal discharge are symptoms of respiratory infections. Inadequate humidity levels or drafts in the enclosure are frequently connected to respiratory illnesses.

External parasites, such as mites, can cause discomfort and worry. Weight loss, diarrhea, and regurgitation can all be caused by internal parasites.

Scale Rot is a bacterial illness that causes discolored or damaged scales, which is generally caused by excessive moisture in the enclosure.

oral Rot: This ailment, also known as stomatitis, is characterized by inflammation and infection of the oral tissues. Poor husbandry, injury, or stress can all contribute to it.

Shedding Problems: Low humidity levels might cause shedding problems such as retained eye caps or bits of lost skin.

Preventive Care Procedures:

Preventive treatment is critical to preserving your corn snake's health. Here are some steps you can do to lower your risk of common health problems:

Maintain Good Husbandry: Keep the cage at the proper temperature and humidity conditions, with a clean substrate and secure hiding locations.

If you have numerous snakes, isolate new recruits before introducing them to existing ones to prevent illness transmission.

Cleaning and disinfecting the enclosure on a regular basis will help to avoid the growth of germs, parasites, and fungal illnesses.

Provide a Balanced Diet: A nutritious and diverse diet benefits your corn snake's general health. Avoid overfeeding or feeding too big prey.

Handle your snake lightly and seldom to reduce stress, especially during feeding or shedding times.

Locating and Choosing a Reptile Veterinarian:

A trustworthy reptile veterinarian is vital for preventative health care. When looking for a vet for your corn snake, consider the following:

Look for Reptile Expertise: Select a veterinarian who has expertise treating reptiles, ideally snakes.

Examine Reviews and suggestions: Seek suggestions from fellow reptile lovers or online forums for reliable reptile physicians in your region.

Visit the Clinic: If feasible, go ahead and examine the veterinarian clinic's facilities and discuss their experience with corn snakes.

Availability of Emergency Services: Confirm that the veterinarian provides emergency services or has a referral mechanism in place for after-hours situations.

Corn Snake Emergency Procedures and First Aid:

Every reptile owner must be prepared for emergencies. While professional veterinarian treatment is usually the best choice, learning basic first aid procedures may help a lot. Here are some first aid and emergency procedures:

Respiratory Distress: If you see indications of respiratory distress, such as wheezing or open-mouth breathing, make sure the enclosure is well ventilated. Seek veterinarian care as soon as possible.

Bite Wounds or Injuries: If your snake gets a bite wound or an injury, wipe the afflicted area with a mild antiseptic solution and keep an eye out for indications of infection. If necessary, seek veterinarian care.

If your snake regurgitates, give it some time to recuperate before attempting to eat again. Look for possible causes such as improper temperatures or handling stress.

Mites: If mites are found, isolate the snake, carefully clean the enclosure, and consult with a veterinarian for suitable treatment.

Shedding Difficulties: If your snake has difficulty shedding, give a damp hide or a shedding box to help the process. Unless absolutely required, avoid manually aiding.

To summarize, preventive health care is critical for your corn snake's well-being. Regular health checks, understanding common health concerns, implementing preventative care measures, locating a reliable reptile doctor, and learning emergency protocols are all critical components of responsible ownership. You may help your corn snake have a longer and happier life by remaining watchful and proactive.

CHAPTER FIVE

TAKING CARE OF AND TAMING YOUR CORN SNAKE

Developing a healthy relationship with your corn snake via correct handling and taming is critical for the snake's well-being as well as your happiness as a pet owner. Understanding corn snake behavior, gradually introducing handling, using suitable procedures, gaining trust, and dealing with aggressiveness or defensive behavior are all important parts of effective snake handling.

Understanding the Behavior of Corn Snakes:

Before beginning to handle corn snakes, it is critical to first understand their natural behavior. Corn snakes are solitary and frequently secretive in their native habitat, navigating and hunting with their excellent sense of smell and heat-sensing pits. They are normally docile, although they, like any other animal, may display protective actions if they feel attacked or agitated.

Corn snakes utilize constriction to control their prey, but this is not an indication of human violence. Corn snakes often become calm and patient when they feel safe and are used to being handled.

Handling Is Introduced Gradually:

It's critical to give a new corn snake time to adjust to its new surroundings when you bring it home. Minimize handling at this time to decrease stress and give the snake time to settle in. You can begin introducing handling whenever the snake looks to be at ease in its enclosure and has developed regular eating and shedding cycles.

Begin with brief sessions and progressively increase the length as the snake grows more acclimated to human interaction. It is critical to approach handling with care and consideration for the snake's unique disposition. Some snakes may be more tolerant by nature, but others may require more time and patient coaxing.

Techniques for Proper Handling:

Proper handling skills are critical for both your and your corn snake's safety. Here's a step-by-step procedure:

Wash Your Hands: Before handling your snake, properly wash your hands to eliminate any smells or residues that might create stress.

Slowly approach the snake: Gently open the enclosure and approach the snake calmly and slowly. Avoid making any rapid movements or loud noises that might frighten the snake.

To offer a sense of security, support the snake's body equally when raising it. Avoid squeezing or forcefully holding.

Handle Midbody: Gently yet securely grasp the snake around the midbody, avoiding the head and tail. To keep the snake from feeling uneasy, support it over its full length.

Avoid Sudden Movements: To avoid frightening the snake, move gently and smoothly. Avoid making quick or jerky movements, which might set off a defensive response.

Maintain Calm: Remain calm and relaxed throughout the handling process. Snakes may detect tension and benefit from a calm disposition.

Limit Handling Time: Keep handling sessions brief, especially at first, to prevent overwhelming the snake. Increase the length gradually as the snake grows more acclimated to the encounter.

How to Build Trust with Your Corn Snake:

Building trust with your corn snake takes time and involves patience and consistency. Here are some suggestions for building trust:

Establish a consistent handling practice to assist the snake develop used to human interaction.

Positive Reinforcement: Link handling to pleasant experiences like eating or exploring. This aids in the formation of good connections with human interaction.

Avoid Using Force or violent Handling tactics: Using force or violent handling tactics might lead to stress and protective responses.

Respect Their Boundaries: Be aware of your snake's body language and respect its boundaries. Return it to its container and try again later if it exhibits indications of stress.

Handle After Feeding: After a meal, certain snakes may be more open to handling since they are less concentrated on potential hazards.

How to Handle Aggression or Defensive Behavior:

Even with cautious handling, there may be times when a corn snake demonstrates protective or aggressive behavior. It is critical to distinguish between defensive behavior, which is a natural reaction to perceived dangers, and violence, which is less prevalent but can occur.

Consider the following if your corn snake exhibits protective behaviors such as hissing, striking, or coiling into a defensive posture:

Examine the atmosphere: Make sure the snake's enclosure has enough hiding locations, suitable temperature gradients, and a secure atmosphere.

Examine for Health Problems: Sudden changes in behavior can sometimes suggest underlying health problems. Consult a reptile veterinarian if you detect chronic defensive behavior.

Limit Stressors: Reduce environmental stressors such as loud noises, abrupt movements, or excessive handling.

In the rare case of true hostility, when the snake actively wants to bite, you must rethink your handling skills and consider consulting with a reptile behavior expert or veterinarian.

Finally, managing and taming your corn snake takes time and involves patience, knowledge, and respect for the snake's natural tendencies. You may form a satisfying and delightful connection with your pet corn snake by introducing handling cautiously, utilizing right procedures, creating trust via positive reinforcement, and being attentive to the snake's comfort. Always approach snake handling with care and a focus on the snake's well-being, creating a pleasant and stress-free atmosphere for both you and your scaly buddy.

CHAPTER SIX

BREEDING AND REPRODUCTION IN CORN SNAKES

Corn snake breeding may be an exciting and gratifying experience for reptile aficionados. Understanding the complexities of corn snake reproduction, selecting good breeding partners, developing a proper breeding habitat, regulating the gestation and egg incubation phase, and caring for hatchlings and juveniles are all important components of successful breeding. In this detailed tutorial, we will look at each of these factors in depth to offer a full understanding of the breeding and reproduction process in corn snakes.

Corn Snake Reproduction Overview:

Corn snakes reproduce sexually, as do many other reptiles. They are oviparous, which means they lay eggs instead of giving birth to live offspring. Corn snakes reproduce in the wild throughout the spring and early summer, with females producing eggs in the summer. Breeders in captivity strive to imitate these natural settings in order to promote effective reproduction.

Environmental conditions, notably temperature, have a significant impact on corn snake reproduction. A chilling phase known as brumation, which replicates the winter months, initiates the female's reproductive cycle. Following this time of cooling, a steady increase in temperature heralds the beginning of the mating season.

Breeding Pair Selection:

Choosing the appropriate breeding couples is an important phase in the breeding process. To guarantee the generation of strong progeny, healthy, well-nourished snakes with no genetic abnormalities should be selected. Breeding pairs should preferably be of comparable size and age, with females at least two years old and males a year or more.

Genetic variety is essential for the offspring's health and vigor. To reduce the chance of genetic defects, avoid breeding close relatives. Keep accurate records of your breeding pairs' ancestry and genetics in order to make educated judgments about future pairings.

Making a Good Breeding Environment:

Setting up a suitable breeding habitat is critical for promoting courtship, copulation, and effective egg laying. Consider the following important factors:

Temperature and Photoperiod: Begin by giving a brumation period during which the snakes are gradually cooled to replicate winter conditions. Gradually raise the temperature and sunshine hours after the brumation phase to simulate spring and initiate the mating season.

Setup an enclosure for the breeding couple, complete with adequate hiding locations and climbing structures. Make sure the enclosure is big enough to fit both snakes comfortably.

Introduction and Courtship: Introduce the male gradually to the female's enclosure. Keep an eye out for indications of courting, such as the male rubbing his chin against the female, coiling around her, or engaging in a dance-like mating ritual. If aggressive behavior is noticed, separate the snakes and reintroduce them later.

Copulation: After a successful courtship, copulation may occur. This can continue several hours, if not days. Multiple copulations may improve the chances of conception.

Following copulation, watch the female for indications of gravidity (pregnancy). For egg laying, provide her with an appropriate nesting box filled with a substrate such as vermiculite or perlite.

Period of Gestation and Egg Incubation:

Corn snakes do not have regular pregnancies; instead, females deposit eggs following a gestation period. The gestation stage, also known as the pre-laying shed, lasts around 28 to 35 days. During this period, the female may experience behavioral changes such as decreased appetite and increased restlessness.

The female will go through a pre-laying shed, during which she will lose her skin in preparation for egg laying. The female will lay a clutch of eggs after this shed. The amount of eggs produced varies depending on characteristics such as the female's age, size, and health.

Once the eggs have been deposited, they must be transferred to an incubator for optimum development. The temperature of the incubation chamber is an important element in determining the sex of the hatchlings. Incubation temperatures of 82-84°F (28-29°C) create a mix of male and female progeny, with slightly lower temperatures producing more females and higher ones producing more males.

Incubation durations are generally 55-60 days long. It is critical to continuously monitor temperature and humidity levels throughout this period to guarantee healthy growth and hatching.

Taking Care of Hatchlings and Juveniles

When the eggs hatch, caring for the hatchlings becomes an important part of the breeding process. Consider the following points:

Separation: After hatching, it is best to separate the hatchlings to avoid cannibalism. Individual enclosures should have suitable hides, water dishes, and heat sources.

Hatchlings can be started on pinky mice of acceptable size. Feeding them should be done with caution, since they may be more fragile than adult snakes. Monitor their weight on a regular basis and change feeding regimens as needed.

Enclosure Size: Gradually increase the size of the hatchlings' cages to allow their growth. To encourage natural behaviors, provide climbing structures and hiding places.

Temperature and Humidity: Keep the snakes at the right temperature and humidity levels for their age. Young snakes may need somewhat more humidity than adults.

Regularly monitor the hatchlings' health, looking for symptoms of sickness, adequate shedding, and normal weight increase. If any health issues emerge, seek veterinarian care.

To summarize, breeding and reproducing corn snakes requires careful planning, attention to environmental conditions, and attentive care for both the adult snakes and their progeny. Selecting breeding couples, creating an appropriate habitat, monitoring gestation and incubation periods, and providing sufficient care for hatchlings are all essential components of successful corn snake reproduction. Breeders may help to the conservation and variety of this popular reptile species by knowing the natural reproductive patterns of corn snakes and applying best practices.

CHAPTER SEVEN

CORN SNAKE ENRICHMENT AND MENTAL STIMULATION

It is critical to provide an enriching and psychologically engaging environment for captive corn snakes. While these reptiles don't have the same amount of interpersonal interaction as mammals, they do have cognitive capacities and innate instincts that may be fostered via intelligent enrichment. We will look at the necessity of enrichment for corn snakes, techniques of providing a stimulating environment, do-ityourself (DIY) enrichment options, detecting behavioral indicators of a content corn snake, and the value of balancing mental and physical well-being in this investigation.

The Importance of Corn Snake Enrichment:

Enrichment is essential for corn snakes because it mimics their natural habits, increases brain stimulation, and enhances general well-being. Corn snakes in the wild engage in behaviors such as climbing, exploring, and hunting. Boredom, frustration, and even health problems can occur in captive situations that lack stimulation.

Mental stimulation is especially helpful for reducing behavioral issues caused by captivity-related stress. Enrichment allows the snake's natural behaviors to be expressed, lowering stress and fostering a happier, healthier pet.

Creating an Exciting Environment

designing a stimulating environment for corn snakes entails designing a habitat that allows for natural activities as well as possibilities for cerebral involvement. Here are several crucial elements:

Corn snakes are skilled climbers, and placing branches or other climbing structures in their habitat encourages them to explore vertical places.

Hiding Places: Hiding places are vital for a snake's mental health. They create a sense of security and resemble the natural refuge locations sought by corn snakes in the wild.

Experiment with various surfaces, such as aspen bedding, cypress mulch, or coconut coir, to give sensory diversity for the snake to investigate.

Environmental modifications: Make modifications to the environment on a regular basis. To avoid boredom, rearrange décor, provide new hiding locations, or change climbing structures.

Feeding Difficulties: Instead of putting food in a bowl, consider hiding it within the cage. This increases the snake's hunting instincts and adds a cerebral component to eating.

DIY Ideas for Enrichment:

DIY enrichment options can bring a creative touch to your corn snake's surroundings. Here are some basic yet powerful suggestions:

fragrance Trails: Make fragrance trails out of non-toxic items such as plants. This stimulates the snake's sense of smell, causing it to follow the path.

Puzzle Feeders: Create simple puzzle feeders out of PVC pipes or other non-hazardous materials. Place food inside, and the snake will have to investigate and find out how to get it out.

Offer empty cardboard boxes of various sizes with apertures for the snake to investigate. This simulates the cramped conditions they could experience in the wild.

Climbing Logs: Attach climbing logs or branches firmly fixed at different levels within the enclosure. This encourages natural climbing.

Sensory Materials: Use non-toxic, safe materials with a variety of textures, such as silk or fabric leaves. Snakes may slither through or rest on various textures to stimulate their senses.

Behavioral Signs of a Satisfied Corn Snake:

Recognizing indicators of happiness in a corn snake is critical for determining the efficiency of the enrichment supplied. The following behaviors are displayed by content snakes:

Exploration: A snake that actively explores its cage, examining different hides, climbing structures, and substrate, is likely to be happy and engaged.

Regular Feeding Response: A healthy feeding response implies that the snake is satisfied. If the snake takes food eagerly and swallows it without hesitation, it indicates a pleasant mental state.

Natural habits: Natural habits including as climbing, basking, and burrowing suggest that the snake is content, which is a good indicator.

Shedding Success: Successful and consistent shedding indicates good health and a supportive environment for the snake's physiological demands.

Corn snakes, like many reptiles, require a basking area on a regular basis. When a snake uses its basking area on a regular basis, it indicates a comfortable and contented habitat.

Managing Mental and Physical Health:

While physical health is critical, mental well-being is as important for a happy and healthy corn snake. Balancing mental and physical well-being entails:

Adequate Space: Make sure the cage is large enough to accommodate the snake's size, allowing for natural activities and exploration.

Proper Nutrition: A well-balanced diet benefits both physical and mental health. Provide a range of prey items and follow a feeding plan appropriate for the snake's age and size.

While not every snake enjoys being handled, certain individuals benefit from moderate and regular engagement. This helps to create trust and stimulates the mind.

Monitoring Stressors: Identify and reduce environmental stressors such as abrupt loud noises, excessive handling, or disturbances to their routine.

Maintain Consistent Environmental Conditions: Keep the temperature and humidity levels steady in order to give a pleasant and predictable habitat for the snake.

To summarize, enriching the habitat and giving mental stimulation for corn snakes is a multidimensional strategy that includes careful enclosure design, DIY enrichment ideas, identifying signals of happiness, and balancing both mental and physical elements of well-being. You may help your pet corn snake's general health, happiness, and lifespan by spending time and ingenuity in providing a stimulating habitat.